W9-BKL-538

SHEAMUS

BY PAUL DINZEO

BELLWETHER MEDIA · MINNEAPOLIS, MN

Are you ready to take it to the extreme?
Torque books thrust you into the action-packed world
of sports, vehicles, mystery, and adventure. These books
may include dirt, smoke, fire, and dangerous stunts.
WARNING : read at your own risk.

Library of Congress Cataloging-in-Publication Data

Dinzeo, Paul.
Sheamus / by Paul Dinzeo.
    p. cm. -- (Torque: Pro Wrestling Champions)
Includes bibliographical references and index.
Summary: "Engaging images accompany information about Sheamus. The combination of high-interest
subject matter and light text is intended for students in grades 3 through 7"--Provided by publisher.
ISBN 978-1-60014-752-4 (hardcover : alk. paper)
1. Sheamus, 1978- 2. Wrestlers--United States--Biography--Juvenile literature. I. Title.
GV1196.S54D56 2012
796.812092--dc23
[B]   2011036522

Printed in the United States of America, North Mankato, MN.

010112   1202

CONTENTS

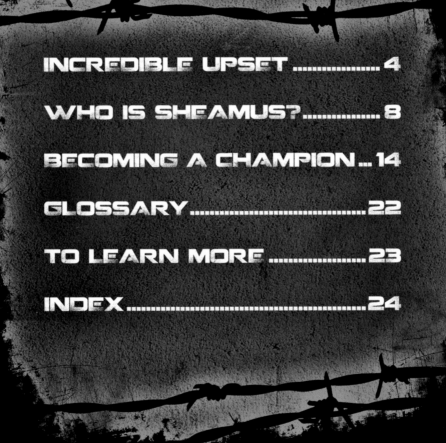

INCREDIBLE UPSET

Sheamus took World Wrestling Entertainment (WWE) by storm in 2009. The big Irish newcomer was unstoppable. In December, he got his chance at the biggest title in wrestling. He stepped into the ring with John Cena to fight for the WWE Championship. It was a **tables match**. The first man to throw his opponent through a table in the ring would win.

JOHN CENA

QUICK HIT!

Sheamus was named WWE's 2009 Breakout Superstar of the Year.

VITAL STATS

Wrestling Name: _____ Sheamus

Real Name: _____ Stephen Farrelly

Height: _____ 6 feet, 4 inches (1.9 meters)

Weight: _____ 267 pounds (121 kilograms)

Started Wrestling: _____ 2002

Finishing Move: _____ High Cross

Cena dominated the beginning of the match. Eventually, Cena had Sheamus on the top rope. He tried to throw him into the table below. Sheamus quickly reversed the move and shoved Cena off the rope. Cena flew backward and smashed through the table. It was over! Sheamus was the new WWE champ!

WHO IS SHEAMUS?

Stephen Farrelly was born on January 28, 1978 in Ireland. He and his family lived in a small town in Dublin. Stephen loved professional wrestling. However, he could not watch matches live on TV. Instead, his dad brought him videotapes of WrestleMania II and III. He watched them over and over.

Stephen was big and athletic. He played **rugby** and **Gaelic football**. By age 16, he worked out almost every day with his father. Stephen later earned a degree from the National College of Ireland. He got a job working at an insurance company in Dublin.

QUICK HIT!

In 2002, Stephen began training at the Monster Factory wrestling school. He learned many moves he now uses in his career.

QUICK HIT!

Sheamus covers himself with sunblock before leaving the house. He wants to be as pale as possible.

Stephen never forgot his childhood dream of becoming a wrestler. He went to England every weekend to wrestle in small leagues. His wrestling names were Sheamus O'Shaunessy and The Celtic Warrior. He quickly became a star in the United Kingdom. In 2007, WWE signed him to a **developmental contract**. He quit his job and headed to the United States.

BECOMING A CHAMPION

WWE sent Sheamus to a small league called Florida Championship Wrestling (FCW). He won the FCW Heavyweight Championship a year later. In June 2009, Sheamus earned a spot in WWE's Extreme Championship Wrestling (ECW). He shortened his name to Sheamus and became a **heel**.

In November 2009, Sheamus won a **break out match**. He earned a shot at the WWE Championship. Sheamus shocked the crowd by beating John Cena. It had taken him less than half a year to rise to the top of WWE! A year later, he won the famous King of the Ring tournament. His popularity made him a **face**.

QUICK HIT!

Sheamus was the first Irish-born WWE Champion.

Sheamus is a force in WWE. Fans know him for his powerful **signature moves**. One of them is the Irish Curse. Sheamus lifts the opponent and slams him down over his knee. To perform the Brogue Kick, Sheamus jumps and kicks his opponent in the face with the bottom of his foot.

Sheamus often uses the High Cross to end a match. This **finishing move** is devastating. Sheamus lifts his opponent above his head. He stretches the opponent's arms so they form the shape of a cross. Finally, he hurls the opponent forward, slamming him into the mat. All that's left is for Sheamus to end the match with a pin. Wrestlers have learned to respect the power of Sheamus, the terror of the Emerald Isle!

HIGH CROSS

break out match—a match in which several wrestlers who have never held a WWE title compete for the right to a championship match

developmental contract—an agreement in which a wrestler signs with WWE but then wrestles in a smaller league to gain experience and develop skills

face—a wrestler seen by fans as a hero

finishing move—a wrestling move meant to finish off an opponent so that he can be pinned

Gaelic football—a team sport that is popular in Ireland; Gaelic football combines elements of soccer, football, and rugby.

heel—a wrestler seen by fans as a villain

rugby—a team sport played with a ball that may be thrown backward, kicked, or carried

signature moves—moves that a wrestler is famous for performing

tables match—a match in which a wrestler wins by forcing his opponent through a table in the ring

TO LEARN MORE

AT THE LIBRARY

Black, Jake. *The Ultimate Guide to WWE.* New York,
N.Y.: Grosset & Dunlap, 2010.

Kaelberer, Angie Peterson. *Cool Pro Wrestling Facts.*
Mankato, Minn.: Capstone Press, 2011.

Stone, Adam. *John Cena.* Minneapolis, Minn.:
Bellwether Media, 2011.

ON THE WEB

Learning more about Sheamus
is as easy as 1, 2, 3.

1. Go to www.factsurfer.com.

2. Enter "Sheamus" into the search box.

3. Click the "Surf" button and you will see a list of
related Web sites.

With factsurfer.com, finding more information
is just a click away.

The images in this book are reproduced through the courtesy of: Picture Perfect / Rex USA, front cover, pp. 14-15; Matt Roberts / ZUMA Press, pp. 4-5; John Smolek, pp. 6; Devin Chen, pp. 8, 9, 12-13; Gallo Images / Stringer / Getty Images, pp. 10-11; David Seto, pp. 16-17, 20-21; George Napolitano / Getty Images, pp. 18-19.